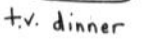

rocket

SAID LIKE REEDS OR THINGS

MARK TRUSCOTT

COACH HOUSE BOOKS

first edition

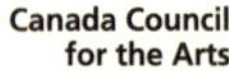

Conseil des Arts
du Canada

Canada

Published with the assistance of the Canada Council for the Arts and the Ontario Arts Council. We also acknowledge the financial support of the Government of Ontario through the Ontario Book Publishing Tax Credit Program and the Government of Canada through the Book Publishing Industry Development Program (BPDIP).

LIBRARY AND ARCHIVES CANADA CATALOGUING IN PUBLICATIONS

Truscott, Mark, 1970–
Said like reeds or things / Mark Truscott. – 1st ed.

Poems.
ISBN 1-55245-145-3

I. – Title.

PS8639.R88S23 2004 C811'.6 C2004-903777-3

for Lisa Heggum
and
to the memory of my grandfather
E. S. Elensky

BIO

It goes on longer and registers
a quarter turn but in reality
continues in a straight line. What's
new in the world? It is
soulful, tender maybe. Have you
seen *Winged Migration*? One of our
cats, Simon, just let out a small
groan, stretched and went
back to sleep. I like Arm & Hammer
better than Crest. What if grass just
grew instead of being subjected to our
need to shape things? No one is afraid
of the honourable-walking-around man.
The game is tied now; it's hard to say who will win.

SAID LIKE REEDS OR THINGS

MYSTERY

Kitchen knife
near table's
edge
                    sun
centred perfectly
in open
window

TRACES

Why
in the afternoon

is the same thought
coloured so

differently?

*

Fence posts leaning
as if in

a strong wind

MID-MORNING

You need to think do you think
the light falling on the floor
through the window through the
trees the branches the leaves
is part of the day around you is
something you can see and
or see by

CYCLE

The trees grow up
and down

the sky, holding

clouds burn
oneiric lines

in the summer
the winter

the road

still walking

SURFACE

The still dark water

the surface of

finally through

rushes pushing

or said like reeds or

things never thought

of thinking saying

from the darkness

that speak softly

whose are the voices

I think after all

Clouds
    edges

just
talking

leaves answer answer leaves

CIRCULARITY

Power
cuts

out

cats
brush

dark
windows

ORNAMENT

bird

sky
or
sky

EXTENSION

one
on
one
no

EXTENDED

one
on
one
or

THING

blank know wonder error orange

NORTH

light lines
limn limbs
lift lids
like light

like light
lifts lids
limbs limn
line light

SOUTH

sudden
curtain
sunlight
outside

HINGE

the lip the
windowsill
white white

FALL

in grass

missed

eyeless

MATTER

flicker

reflection

ONTOLOGY

It's thcre.

SERIES

realize
realign
realize

WINTER

Knowing he's dead, Glenn Gould plays Schoenberg.
Knowing he's dead, Glenn Gould plays Schoenberg.

WAVE

Yeah each way was still lit.

NEGATIVE

Oh, it
snowed.

FOUND

The room was full of people picking their noses.
The room was full of people picking their nose.

FOUNDER

Reality is heterogeneous.

INSTABILITY

This:

is

it. It

A POSITION

This, a
little
death.

HAIKU

like

mpty so what
is it

sounds

PASTORAL

where or
only odd
dolmen

QUIET

pipe   or a
along
occasion

IT'S

new window

excite exact

SOUND

audio or our ouroboros

SOUNDING

odd eolith ogre aphesis

WORKSHOP

whatelse
thatsome
      play

LINES

no one saw our narrow vision move across

VALUE

What if it's
consonant

EQUALS

a ha agh ha ha

UNTITLED

so so so

FEEL

so so so

FUCK

Image is seven.

NOVEMBER 1

close a
dark
wind
wall
stutters

NOVEMBER 2

ATMS on
rain
grade
sputum
streets

HAP

a one
an on

SONG

one a
or our
an or
and an

SING

an and or our
or an ATM

GEOMETRY

postcards windows
outside shelves
through anyone moving
boxes there think
could look open
still your bed

in of on

COMMON

Air: alone:
you are

outlines:

glass:
the dust

dances
the window

sun
struck

moment, airily
opaque

as this
pen, these

somnambulant
fingers

IT'S SNOWING

CANADIAN POETRY

It's true, air conditioning
makes you feel more in control.
The grass between tents at the picnic
is getting worn down. Prepositions
pass the muster. Lisa
passes the salt. Who
will tip the waiter?
Bush speaks urgently in the Rose Garden.
Misunderstanding is its own reward.

BUM CIRCUITS

Egg in the face of your favourite statue. Was that you in the cool lemon hallway? I always thought I couldn't really think. The ink of the current notion had just dried when it was proven false. What else was he to do in light of all the focus groups? The loops of orange, green and blue were of their own intelligence but seemed to allude to something medical and perhaps in some sense then obscene. The leaning tree wasn't really symbolic of anything as it caught the rusty light. The slight tremor arose in spite of the currents being absolutely still. She will leave the room by the door through which he entered. The centre of the causeway was likewise an imposition. The partition fell the very moment the counsel dropped her glove. I strove always to mind my connotations and create a good impression. The succession of torn envelopes was all we had in mind and all there was.

SNOW

It's
snow
ing

Inside hollow tire sounds I'm
careful with sentences

Who *isn't* knocking?

Accumulating
mechanisms built into
their surroundings

The dryer isn't
 lonely any more

People trip
over themselves

No one screws with
this operating system

The light on
in and out

LIFESTYLES

O can I say

the levelling
of first persons

Thirteen
is a great deal

What do you think
of that smell

He then took up
the remainder to dispense with it

To consider and the majority
are involuntary

To glance and the surface
is flavourless

To count and the credit
is insoluble

That's why we scratch
and skip

SOME MORNINGS I MISTRUST SYNTHESIS

What is it if it establishes a closeness
I am happy about ringing but wary of imposition
True the pencil is close in my hand
True I imagine various elements sharing a common
    participant
The limit of resonance is the fading that reveals
My participation scratches it scratches
In the white field what is it rings like a bell

EIGHTS

1)

To say it is lateral, unhanded, ultimately multiple and
therefore frivolous

While driving with one hand, with the other she rolled
the window down

Speaking, and the fingers find the hair among the teeth

A memory that is at the same time an exploration and a
distraction

Considering the relationship of history to classic rock

She voted Liberal for fear the Alliance would win

The scratches in the paint seemed to aspire to a minor
literature

Which is to say they too were immanent as the grass
spread every which way

2)

The room then is taken in in sections

Configuration is dependent on an external apparatus

Who tends to ward off intrusions is therefore a slovenly architect

There were poles beside the roadway, each with a numbered indication

Just then she felt her eyes mirrored by other, external eyes

The CBC logo has recently changed from multicoloured opacity to digital, clearer-than-clear, 'gelled' transparency

The crisis of influence is an example of the rebellion against the tendency toward homogeneity

Each check of the mirror began another age

3)

One is puzzled by a room's odd assortment

Thirteen objects unarranged but in close proximity, which are therefore static, and the space they occupy, wide

He liked sometimes to refer to his various reliable ideas as his bag of tricks

Two people walked side by side with no present calling beyond those that were part of their own accumulated definitions

Three people walk the same way

There is no inherent impetus to addition

I was thinking of a collection that acknowledges that to add is sometimes to reduce

That thinks about the difference between addition and accumulation

4)

The bored security guard was trying to imagine a practicable utopia

He was apart from the building's other inhabitants, some of whom, because of the difference in economic status they perceived, considered him of a lower order

He was spinning his Hawaii key chain on a raised index finger

The grass in a previous section is still spreading and likewise extending upward, even after all this time

The cool repetition of strangers

The mind stopping and starting how many times

The people in the next building went about their business as ever before, separated as they were by a world-ending thick wall

Shadows and white light stuttered as headlights count an odd number of concrete walls

WHIP

Everything I say is
difficult to say where
it starts on the sign saying
come in we are open
ended before it started
saying you're syn-
chronic aren't you
going to open it isn't
accounted for either you
ride past tense power
lines appearing around
narrowed eyes

SCHOOLS

It's all loosely fitted together the way
real messes aren't at all stylish. The
guy on my street we call the Chump
is probably headed for something different
and less total than he's hoping for.
The mould I thought I smelled is actually
the slightly brown bananas over the sink
and they're still life. I read somewhere
that dialectics are out and that it's all free
radicals now. No one tells you when you're
disarmingly average. Everyone wants a
bungling sidekick. How am I supposed to write
when there's always something on TV?

IT WAS

It was hot I saw.

Like light on rain on the road at night.

Notice its
i

it's like
its like.

The shade had shadow.

flash
show what
Watt

leaf

The heat.
A hat.

The note.
A knot.

A not.

It seemed this was it.

Mark Truscott was born in Bloomington, Indiana, but has spent most of his life in Canada. He has had poems published in a number of magazines, including *filling Station, The Literary Review of Canada, The Malahat Review, Peter O'Toole* and *This Magazine*. He lives in Toronto.

Please visit www.saidlikereedsorthings.ca.

ACKNOWLEDGEMENTS

Thanks to my family, especially my dad, who taught me to read, and my mom, who taught me to interrogate language. Thanks to Bill Minor and Lisa Jarnot, each of whom cleared paths.

Thanks to Jay Millar and Alana Wilcox, to Jay for his sensitive and respectful editing and to Alana for believing in my writing for a while now. Thanks to Darren Wershler-Henry for his thoughtful design. Thanks to Jason McBride, Christina Palassio, Stan Bevington and all at Coach House.

Thanks to the Ontario Arts Council and the Canada Council for the Arts for the money. Thanks to the Banff Centre for the Arts for the Wired Writing Studio and for hooking me up with Don Domanski. Thanks to him, too.

Thanks to Nelson Ball, all at Book City, Christine Dalgetty, Joanne Hawthorne, Pat Magosse, Krista Philbrick, Stuart Ross and Ania Szado.

Thanks to the editors of *The Antigonish Review, Fiddlehead, filling Station, The Literary Review of Canada, The Malahat Review* and *This Magazine,* who published poems from this book, often in earlier and radically different form. 'Winter' and 'Pastoral' appeared in the BookThug anthology *Pissing Ice.*

Most, thanks and love to Lisa Heggum, my companion on this and that side of language.

Typeset in Centaur and Household Items
Printed and bound at the Coach House
on bpNichol Lane, 2004

Edited by Jay Millar
Copy edited by Alana Wilcox
Designed by Darren Wershler-Henry

Coach House Books
401 Huron Street (rear) on bpNichol Lane
Toronto, Ontario
M5S 2G5

416 979 2217
1 800 367 6360

mail@chbooks.com
www.chbooks.com